SOUL SONGS

ALSO BY GUNILLA NORRIS

Books on the Spirituality of the Everyday

Being Home: A Book of Meditations
Becoming Bread: Meditations on Loving and Transformation
Inviting Silence: Universal Principles of Meditation
A Mystic Garden: Working with Soil, Attending to Soul
Simple Ways: Towards the Sacred
Embracing the Seasons: Memories of a Country Garden
Sheltered in the Heart: Spirituality in Deep Friendship
Match: Bringing Heart and Will into Alignment
Companions on the Way: A Little Book of Heart-full Practices
Touched by Blessing
On the Wing: A Book of Days
Great Love in Little Ways: Reflections on the Power of Kindness
Care and Prayer: Reflections on the Sacred Task of Caregiving
The Light of Evening: Meditations on Growing in Old Age
Discerning with the Heart: Praying for Guidance and Vision

Books of Poetry

Learning from the Angel
Joy is the Thinnest Layer
Calling the Creatures
Old and Singing

SOUL SONGS

A Strand of Praise

Gunilla Norris

BOOK PUBLISHING COMPANY
RHINEBECK, NEW YORK

Paperback ISBN 9781958972847
eBook ISBN 9781958972854

Library of Congress Cataloging-in-Publication Data

Names: Norris, Gunilla, 1939- author.
Title: Soul songs : a strand of praise / Gunilla Norris.
Description: Rhinebeck, New York : Monkfish Book Publishing Company, 2025.
Identifiers: LCCN 2025011826 (print) | LCCN 2025011827 (ebook) | ISBN 9781958972847 (paperback) | ISBN 9781958972854 (ebook)
Subjects: LCGFT: Poetry.
Classification: LCC PS3564.O646 S68 2025 (print) | LCC PS3564.O646 (ebook) | DDC 811/.54--dc23/eng/20250404
LC record available at https://lccn.loc.gov/2025011826
LC ebook record available at https://lccn.loc.gov/2025011827

Book design by Greta Sibley
Illustrations by Iris Morton
Cover design by Colin Rolfe

Monkfish Book Publishing Company
22 East Market Street, Suite 304
Rhinebeck, New York 12572
(845) 876-4861
monkfishpublishing.com

INTRODUCTION

Sometimes in deep quiet a few words will come
as if a bead were dropped into my hands,
something to hold and experience. Why those words?
There is no answer other than to receive
what might come on any given day and to allow it
to infuse and inform me.

The day's words join other words from other days
as if they were prayer beads on a string.
Perhaps in simple recognition
they become a way to be closer
to the Holy One that is near
and yet far beyond words.

Often I experience that there is no song inside me.
Then I know it is time to tune to the One
I call You and wait
until I remember that whether I sing
my soul songs or not,
I am still living their notes
and the spaces that open between them

Beginning

It's early Morning
The street is silent.

The day waits
or seems to be waiting.
I close my eyes.

The flood tide of prayer
rises and swells . . .

a way to be near You
and yet it's not You.

Only You
will bring me to You.

I

The smallest thing will not be forgotten

– Julian of Norwich

One morning early
with dawn not yet, I heard,

Be soft.
Be dark.
Let quiet come
and linger.

Let in the hidden light
your eyes can't see.

Now soft.
Now dark.
I am that self same
dark but darker

and will unfold a dawn
of growing light.

You have entered,
dear quiet,
through the gap
at the bottom of the door

. . . so small,
silent and on tip toe
coming close
offering yourself.

I feel you in my lap
as night falls
and lights diminish
and wink out in the street.

I know you are naked,
ask for nothing and are
simply here. Will you let me
be your manger full of straw?

Oh, that I could
learn to live
in a small
sacred way
as a keyhole,
a hollow reed,
a window, or
a buttonhole.
Might I then
find a place
of belonging
amongst all
the ways
You shower me
with openings
that lead to You
and Your closures.

The daily tasks
are myriad and
of no account –

wash, dress, eat,
tend and live
the simplest.

Why question
what I do or
if I'm worthy?

Would we question
thistles or the soft, white
fragrance of the lily?

Outside
the snow is falling.
Inside
I count beads
on my necklace
wanting something
to hold
that won't disappear
as if fingering
a string
of blue baubles
could begin
to be better
than the soft
layering of
the world
with an always
about-to-melt
beauty.

There is no hiding,
only becoming. Deeper
than I can know
is a simple doorway.

I am always walking
toward it. Will I find You
beyond the threshold?

Or is it You who took
my hand and all this time
has walked me toward it?

There's a shyness
of soul that wants
not to hide
but to be
allowed to stand
on the threshold
where inside
and outside
embrace and converse
as if they were
long-lost friends
and the soul comes
as close as it dares
to listen, to listen
again and again.

Invited
into morning
I will be
sent back to evening.

There, between
two nights, You are
the love-hinge
that greets me

at the door
as it opens
and closes, as it
infinitely swings.

I felt You
brush by me,
so close You took
my plum-colored shawl.

Were You wind, breath,
a thief that left me
naked and filled
with strange longing?

Not alone
in my sorrows.

You are there
with my tears.

All that I love,
You love as well.

All that's fallen
into ruin is

with You –
not forgotten.

Can it be that from You,
daring comes

for my heart
to hold more?

Finally
after many years
something small slips
in, knows how to nestle
close between breaths,
between each heart beat
and whispers me into being
the one I already am. Yours.
Shy in Your darkness, I feel
my heart break and open.

The flame
in my candle
leaps in the dark.

With a hand
near the heat
I ask to be lit

to burn, to melt
what there is
of leftover wax.

No one is
without its other.
We are together
tender and helpless,
side by side
while Your love does
what it does . . .
drenching us
in sweetness
wrenching us
in pain. You join
us to all we want
to think of as other.

Can I let go
of the me that caused
the pains that left
a trail of thorny hurts
and large betrayals?

Abandon her?
Leave her for the one
I really am – defenseless,
and bare, stepping out
from behind shadows.

Can I leave that self
without a shred of shame?
That is love's story.
You offer me tomorrow
and beginning again.

Your angel said,
Come slowly
to the smallest yearning
waiting inside you.

Come slowly and
with a tender hand
touch what waits for
recognition.

Come slowly,
as if your walking
could make a bridge
to what is too new
to be born today.

Come slowly.
What is small
and helpless is
already blending with
not yet and soon to be.

Do you see
how the wind rocks
the empty rocker
out there
on the splintering pier
whose weathered pilings
reach into deep water?

The rocker rocks.
A crow sweeps by as if
it was flowing ink
drawn across an empty page.
Perhaps something is asking
to be named?

The squeak and rustle
of the rocker is gentle,
a mothering sound. Surely
it's a lullaby for something
so fragile, so new it cannot bear
to know it's been noticed.

The cradle
of your silence
rocks me.

Love-lulled
I'm small,
so small, so
very small.

I was invisible until
You named me.

Now I am a speck,
a self so insignificant

it seems I am near
to nothing.

Yet I have Your gift
of wings.

You never tell
a fly to fly.

It somehow does
on iridescent wings.

Quietly fumbling
and with a roaring
river inside
I want to pray.

Tongue-tied, I gaze
down to the floor
as praise rises in my chest
banging for release.

Under the bed
a pair of old shoes
waits for me
to walk out of myself.

Out of the crack
in the concrete,
out of the felled
and decimated tree,
in my stormy soul,
a little thing
springs forth . . .

green,
audacious,
unabashed,
of no account
and yet real.

How faithless
to think
I've invented this
brazen boldness,
this unearned joy!

II

Your desire is infinite
and everything that proceeds from that desire –
your love, your tears, your hopes –
become infinite as they must be
if they are to reach Me,
if they are to live.

– Catherine of Siena

Morning when I wake
my throat burns.
I called You all night.
In my sleep You seemed
very close. I want to believe
You are almost here.

Is it better to be hungry
since looking for satisfaction
I might lose all? Is it better
to be lean as an ally cat
whose rib cage ripples
as it yowls?

Strung across the river
is the taut rope of love
and farewell. It shudders
in the passing winds.

I beg angels for footing.

I teeter and shake, shout
and wail, inching across
the abyss toward acceptance
and what I want to believe

to be shore . . . perhaps shore.

Push me
past
the rock pile
of endless excuses.

Push me past
the lip of fear,
the gray dam
of reluctance.

Push me
into unbounded
fathoms of mercy.
Fell me.

Like a stone
dropped into silence
in a running river

I sink.

Water rushes over me.

I sink.

The bottom falls away.

I sink

and disappear
in waters
without beginning,

without end.
Can this be Your Love?

What enters the heart?
Many things. They are
everywhere waiting
to graze the softness
of the waiting body –

beauty that once was and can
no longer be. Love-fragrance
that seeps out of a misaddressed
letter. The friend that left

without saying goodbye.
A tree in full bloom
fell all at once
when the moon was full.

Even before we existed,
suffering was waiting
to make something of us,
to ripen our acceptance.

When I won't wait
for You and
drum ten fingers
on the slow
progression of
sought for dreams
and hopes for
their fruition,
I refuse to ripen.
I live haste,
that hot house
scourge of hurry
and emptiness.
I do not grow
into the slow
becoming
You want for me –
that sovereign ease.

How many times
do I say, Lord or
Good Lord or
Your Majesty
and push You away
on the gilded throne
I have given You?

With You at a distance,
I feel safe.
Your love scares me.
I toss salt over
my shoulder, in case . . .

How invisible
and deeply You are
within – no distance,
no measure. Already
You're too close for me
to see or to feel You.

Toss in wood,
toss in paper,
fan them into flame –
let things be
as they are
and burn inside me.
That fire will leap
and caper
until it goes out
as it should,
as it should,
for then darkness
will not scare me.
I'll sit in a room,
perhaps it's today,
strangely warmed
by kindling
gently laid again
on the cold hearth
of my heart.

There is a fire
I have known
lying down
heavy and solid
as a piece of wood,
a lost part of the forest.

Under me
hearth stones.
Above me, the flue
open where a little sliver
of the sky enters as if
from far away.

Unlit waiting
burns without scarring.
Every want is consumed.
My fears turn white,
then soft and gray . . .
a handful of ashes.

Falling again, I sense
You expect me, and that

I will fall toward You
forever.

Glinting gateways fly past me.
I keep falling.

Your breath comes closer.
It is a flint to my failings.

You light them,
kindle and kiss them,

make them a candelabra
with candles burning.

Always there
when one things ends
and another begins

You are the In-Between
squandering time
in flagrant opulence
that makes things
somehow eternal.

Was I wrong
taking the path
away instead of toward?

Was I wrong
to shun my sorrows,
forget to kiss them?

Was I wrong
to close my eyes
when You stood by me?

How was I wrong
when every path still
takes me toward You?

I trot about
from here
to there
adorned
with sparkling
ornaments.

I prance
in self-made
busyness
while the truth
whispers, smiles
and quietly tells me,

Dear Heart,
do not forget
even a mule
arrayed with
sparkling jewels
is still a mule.

Since You love me,
my footprints in the sand
sift back to their beginning,

to nothing. I travel
as a cloud does, wispy
as a mare's tail trusting

air to hold me as I lift,
shred and tatter
in a widening sky.

Is it time to give
myself back,
to want no thing,

only You? This is the desire
you dreamed for me
out of silence.

What simple task then
to walk from here to here,

walking in circles
yearning for You.

With each footfall my feet learn
by going where they need to go . . .

Disturbance, I need
the kind that brings bees
out of their hives
protecting their queen.

Disturbance, I need you
to show me what I shield
with comings and goings,
and the thoughtless ways
I squander what's given.

Disturbance, I need you
for something to be
born within me. And
if not, subdue me,
enough to bear the ache
of all that lies
unused inside me.

Every moment
and in ecstasy,
You are groaning
on a birthing bed.
Sweat pours from You
in rivers of rain.
No one is there
to console You.
In Your straining,
longing enters us,
and is conceived.
Now we can't help
but carry You –
our little portion
to deliver while You
bear the weight of
endless worlds to come.

There is then
a luminous thread,
such as a spider might
spin from its center,
something sheer
and tensile
that carries us
across days,
spanning one thing
to the next, unfolding
everything that is
meant to happen
between us and You,
between our suffering
and Your love.

You are the one
yearning
inside us and
beside us.

You hold
the wet cord
tied to the bucket
as it strains
into the well,
into the depths
of ache and thirst.
We want to believe
You ache for us also.

Morning stars
shine above
and here below
they glitter
on the dark surface
of the water in the well.

We know that even the light
within us is not ours,
only Yours in reflection.

If I stay
in my self-made desert
long enough,
    if I stay
with sand and the litter
of crumbling stones,
    if I stay
with cacti and nothing
on the horizon,
    if I stay
long enough, will I not
come to what I need –
    the trust
that You are my water
and my thirst.

Arriving
in boundless
and colorful habits
of Being

how do I honor
Your every appearance?
Impossible!
You are too many,

but I hear You
in a foreign tongue
whispering
Allow. Allow.

Pitted
white against black,
rich against poor,
old against young,
insistent walls rise
up between us.

Soften us
into gray that we
may grow light
as the wing-
feathers of a dove
and share Your sky.

All the songs
we sing in our pain,
are not the loud ones,
but the ones that resolve
like chords in the blood
and vibrate our heart valves,

the flesh wings You gave us,
opening and closing,
that we might lift
our spirits and return
again and again to You,
to Your infinite body.

What comforts
and helps?
Nothing.
Uttermost longing
is only answered
by no thing.

Even beauty
when it arrives
fades to nothing.
What is left?
Nothing unfolding,
opening,

dreaming,
becoming
that which makes us
Yours and
far beyond
something.

Difficulty,
I give myself over
to You once more,
that I might ripen
into trust.
How much more
before there is
no more to give?

I don't count fingers
or breaths. My heart
beats, captive to
whatever comes –
desolation, loss, love –
all of it reveals You.
Your Presence is not lost
for You never divide
Yourself from Yourself.

Daybreak,
and in confusion
I'm awake full of fear.

What am I to do?
How am I to be?

A tender sense
of your hand comes
to touch and assure me.

Take heart.
There is no yesterday,
no tomorrow,
only the dawn
of this very day.

How deep this
daring to receive
whatever comes,
and to hold it,
fingers spread as if
they were five feathers.
Lightness fills my palms.

Am I trusted at last
to be a simple place
for love,
my hands a perch
where longing grows
its wings?

Each of us
is given a secret
destination
that unfolds
day by day
without our ken.

We traipse
like pilgrims toward
what we've heard
or think is good,
something imagined
as holy.

At evening,
tired of treading,
You meet us
by the road –
our pilgrim's end
though we don't know
or understand it.

Each day I live within
a seeming compass,

under glass tending
the red arrow

as it swirls
back and forth

up and down
around its center.

You do not ask me
to navigate

but to love and
bear this circling,

this abject, tender,
continual abiding.

You are the point
of the pen. You are
the dripping
from the dishrag.

You are the eyes
that gaze down
and see me without
my usual defenses.

You take my burdens,
and fling them in the ditch.
They are bittersweet now,
wild and free in the mire.

III

A fountain is of no use to someone
who knows of it
but doesn't come to drink its waters.
You must approach if you wish to drink.
– Hildegard of Bingen

Last night
another dusting
came. Snow
whispered down
and killing frost
turned winter berries
into small red lanterns
glowing in the thickets,
showing me an inner way

to be charged
by the cold sting
of the world,
allowing hoar frost
to be the darkness
that renders glimpses
of Your radiance
burning among brambles.

Slant-wise
at the casement,
winter pounds
and storms.
The wind shakes
every fastening.
All night the wild
psalm of it howls.
I lie still
breathing, breathing
the sacred bedlam . . .
the unimpeded glory.

It can be dangerous
to speak, for doesn't it
often turn words
into houses of stone
too cold to live in?

Perhaps it's warmer
outside in the snow and
in heart-rending change.

Perhaps better to feel
the falling flakes instead,
and to burrow
into their layers –
their infinite silence.

Emptiness widens
within me like a river
and moves
past frost-riddled banks.

I step to the edge
hip-high
in cold streaming.
I feel emptiness

tug at me, fiercely
demanding I trust it
to carry me, even as I am
clothed in too much.

Again wet snow
in April. I thought
I was through
with cold
and my soul shivering
in never-ending winter.

But then, I see that
the robin is out
in the slosh and
burgeoning grass
pulling worms from
a cold, holy darkness.

Beyond the window
I hear gulls mewling
as if they were
counting sorrows.

I hear the neighbor's
dog mournfully bark.
It wants to be let in
and belong again.

Patience is
muscular and wrestles
complaints
to the ground

pinning me
down to earth,
making me kinder –
that long, sweaty work.

Today again
I know nothing,
but I sense
the way
the morning fog
caresses the deep
green junipers
and wraps around
the mailbox where
this moment's
truth waits
like an unopened
letter delivered
to me.

I ask You to
take me
  to Your garden
where crabgrass and
  roses are
equal in beauty.

I ask You to
take me
  to Your garden
where thorns glisten
  and berries
ripen with life.

I ask You to
plant me
  in Your garden.
where love is soil.
  Give me roots
to drink Your living water.

The spring
in the rocky wall
pours over granite –
a glistening stream.
The wall, much more
than stone, is where
joy runs rampant,
not worried about
being too much,
not enough,
unwanted or craved.
Your splendor streams
out to all who come
begging to be soaked
in communion.

From the wood lot
I smell the fragrance
of the wild
geraniums
softly rising
as if the ground
were whispering
its longing,
shyly asking
for permission
to wrap the air
with love.
Is it You
making love
out of love?

Words hide You
and yet . . .
without description
would revelation come?
Words hide You
but when . . .
the osprey leaves its nest
and spreads its wings
floating free
like a flying hymn,
You are that swooping,
that wordless grace.

Crows caw.
Dogs bark.
The wind whistles
through the trees
leafing out.

No words contain You.

A child sings.
An old man laughs
Gulls cry . . .
they are words
that hide You

and yet they reveal You.

The susurrus of tides,
the singing thrush,
the hum of stars.
Your love has become
music and language.

When You are near me
grass hums,
babies croon,
peaches ripen, worms
fatten in the ground.

When You are near me
bees drone, larks lift,
old ones smile,
my heart breaks
into glittering pieces.

In their small containers
the moonflower seedlings
look bent like old men
in dun-colored casings.
Shedding protection,
transparent stems rise
slender and fragile.

A blossom will open
one future evening,
white and fragrant,
larger than a child's hand.
It will stretch and reach
the way souls do
wanting something to hold.

From the beginning
it seems
the poppy accepts
its days will be short,
that its inner velvet,
its purple darkness,
will open and expand –
a sky with star-seeds
to scatter. Unrequited
and enduring,
it surrenders,
gives every petal away,
lets them drop like
fluttering flames.

Wrenched sideways
by wind, the tree toppled.
Earth erupted and gaped.
Dun-colored roots rose,
thick as arms. Wet soil
clung to them looking like offal.

Those roots never asked
to be seen, the way hidden
ones who pray for the world
never ask for anything
but to live in Your secrets
and silence.

It was a fissure
in time
when the goldfinch
lighted on the ledge
even though
I was there, close
by the window –
a clumsy sentinel –
where air from outside
could touch me.

Black eyes gazed
through me.
Your creature lingered,
didn't fly, and I wanted
to believe it was there
to show me how.

I sit down
to notice
how rushing
has been emptied
of wind.
It is then
that I hear
Your songs
in birds
as they chatter,
as if preparing
a homecoming
I'm allowed
to attend
if I'll come
wearing feathers.

So many lovely truths
lie scattered
around me – well worn
and rounded like stones
on a beach, washed
over and over.

So many for the taking!
I fill my pockets to bursting,
limp home to make cairns
along the sills of my windows.
Soon the stones turn dusty

and dull. What am I keeping?
Will I not trust that I'll always
have them freely scattered
there on the beach,
washed over, wet, wordless,
sunlit and gleaming?

Once I escaped
both within
and without,
I was sky and earth –
a silent communion.

At my feet
mushrooms raised
their white domes,
their earth mosques
toward heaven.

It was a call to prayer

I heard the jubilee
in fallen leaves, a wet chorus
rising from the ground.
Up was down. Down was up,
joined and the same.

Did I ever think
I knew what
to pray for?
It seems better
to be a tree stump
at the beginning
of the trail
waiting for rain,
waiting
to crumble slowly
for as many seasons
as it takes
to be content
just here, where
an alleluia
of sweet ferns
has grown up
around me.
I am steeped
in their closeness,
their fragrance,
their faith in silence.

Vast as a field
without fences
You wait for us –
endless and patient.

We stand at
hesitation's turnstile
shifting from one foot
to the other. We stand

confused and fearful
like lowing cattle
waiting to be milked.
We wait, not knowing

that You wait for us
where no gate is, giving us
a fearful freedom that
will not be taken from us.

My heart whispers,
        Come
friends and be with me
where grasses are tall
and green with athletic joy.
        Come
where insects sing
their sky-songs, humming
hymns no one has heard.
        Come,
let's stand in this meadow
of sheer permission
while distant trees hold
the field in their branches.
        Come,
we are invited to sit
below leaves in the shade
where there is room for hurts,
the unloved and not yet forgiven.
        Come
where what waits
for us is the gift
that makes us one,
belonging to each other.

Here, on this woodland path
buttercups glow like stars
that bloomed out of darkness.
They are the ground's galaxy.

If they light anyone's way,
they don't care –
a heavenly indifference
that allows me to pick one

and hold it close under your chin,
to see you, dear friend, illumined
in gold. Walking toward the center,
would we ever want more?

I will not wash the apple
in my hand or peel it.
I hold its rosy speckled
weight and feel late spring
and the entire summer.

I roll it in my hands,
and think of Eve and how
small acts of betrayal
can sever everything.
I bite. I bite down hard.

Juice bursts like a shower
or a shaft of light. My mouth
swirls with sweetness and
the tart taste of forgiveness,
the gift of amen.

Being friends
let us not mourn.
Have we not loved,
laughed and lived,
eaten ripe cherries
letting pits fall on the lawn,
felt sun warm our skins?
Did we not touch
what was near and
hidden in broad daylight?
Don't mourn.
Let death be a last,
hallowed gift,
the freedom
that lets things be
exactly as they are.

On a branch
an aspen leaf swivels
as if it were a poem
rendered green
by the sap rising
from darkness
to become
a song singing
to the little cloud
that just now
passed over us
in the blazing blue.

Could I unfurl,
branch and leaf out . . .
greening in spring,
blooming in summer,
dropping simply one day
hearing the song
that sings to itself
for itself
in the blazing blue?

There's passion
in the marrow

of my bones
that click with rhythm

as I dance across
the thread-bare carpet,

the weave of a worn
and lovely life, a ground

whose weft and woof
was woven out of things

I learned to love at last
as they came and went,

one by one, good and bad,
in the swing of things.

The fiestas of Your zinnias
rustle and make music.

Marigolds blaze yellow –
a hundred golden suns.

The green ferns drum. Listen,
the red geraniums are shaking

their crazed castanets. Tell me
if there's a better way than dancing.

Let me arrive at last
without lessons
or confessions.
Together may we come
to a simple trust,
a child's faith,
stroking
its mother's cheeks,
pummeling her breasts
like dough
with abandon
and rapture,
grasping
with all ten fingers
for a foot hold
to climb the torso
of the world
knowing there is
a place in the lap
of goodness
where love flows
like a fountain?
It does. It flows,
and we will drink
and drink our fill.

Ending

I sing to You, Life of my life,
beyond goals or comprehension.
Trackless immensity,
words will never describe You
and yet
in intimate silence
You tenderly come
to the side of the smallest hope,
to the love-ache within,
to the hearts that wait for You.

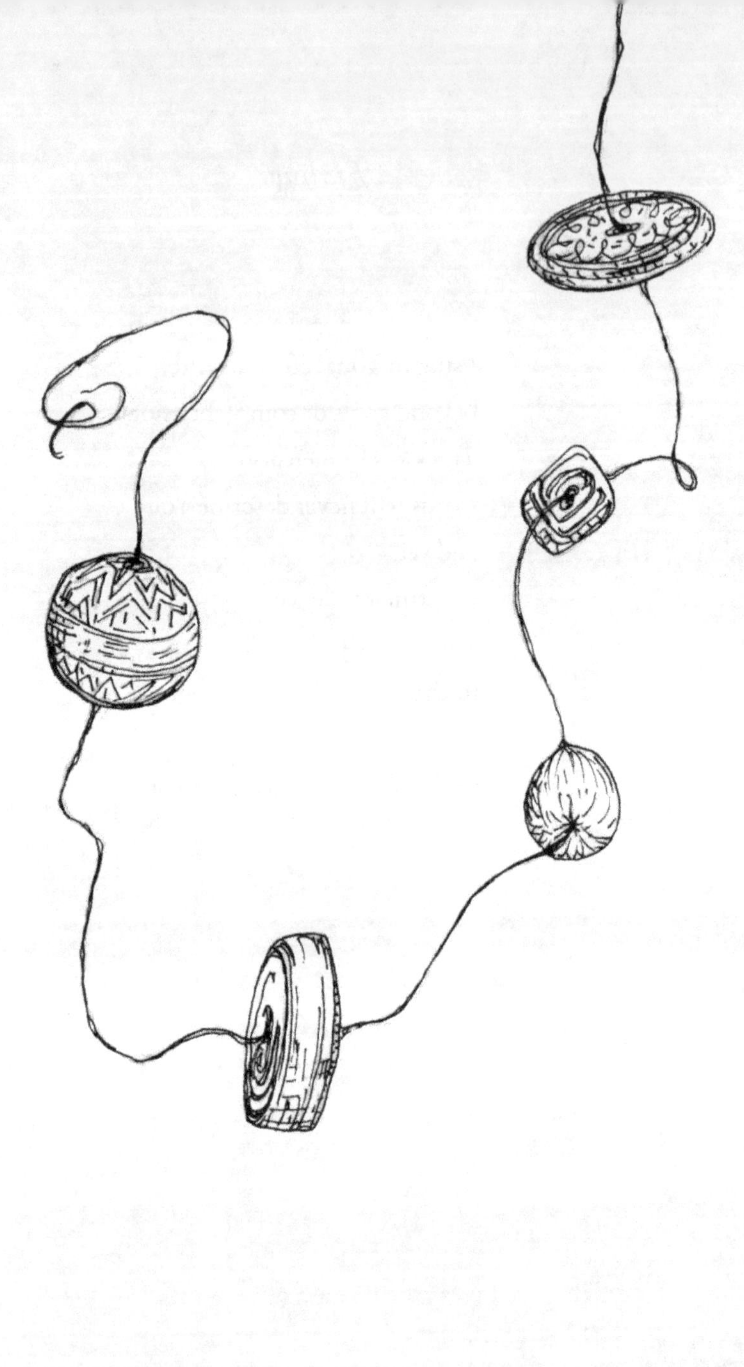

Between God and the soul . . .

there is no between

– Julian of Norwich

ACKNOWLEDGMENTS

Grateful appreciation goes to my friends, Greta Sibley, who beautifully designed and formatted the interior of *Soul Songs* and to Iris Morton for her wonderful, delicate bead drawings.

Support for and suggestions to improve the manuscript have come from dear friends and family: my son, John Norris, Mary Carol Kendzia who was the first to read the manuscript, Danit Fried, Joyce Sievers and Frank Pendola. You gave me courage to continue working on the book. I am so grateful to you.

www.ingramcontent.com/pod-product-compliance
Lightning Source LLC
Jackson TN
JSHW020033150625
85605JS00001B/1

* 9 7 8 1 9 5 8 9 7 2 8 4 7 *